A THRILL OF

Hope

A HIGHLY FAVOURED CHRISTMAS DEVOTIONAL

ISBN:
978-1-967189-24-3 (paperback)
978-1-967189-25-0 (hardback)

Table of Contents

Introduction

Luke 2:19 says, "But Mary kept all these things, and pondered them in her heart." Mary watched in wonder as the events of the first Christmas played out in real time. After a day of travel, giving birth, and a visit from the shepherds, I'm sure Mary was worn out. Yet, as the shepherds left the manger that night, she chose to ponder this miraculous, amazing event! She did not understand everything surrounding Christ's birth, but she certainly meditated on what God had done. She thought it all over carefully, allowing it to sink deep inside her, changing her forever.

Christmas seems to be one of the busiest times of the year! In our efforts to make the holiday special, we rush around participating in so many festive activities that we often find ourselves exhausted and missing out on the true Wonder of the season. Little eyes are watching you. What are they learning about Christmas by how we are acting? Are we teaching them the wonder that God miraculously sent His Son to earth? Or are they only seeing the materialistic side of activities and presents?

So often, the Christmas story becomes something we just read this time of year because it is tradition. We do not put much thought into it; therefore, it does not change us. Oh, that this Christmas we would be like Mary and step aside from the hustle and bustle to meditate on the wonder of Christ's birth! Consider the miracle and purpose of His coming and the fulfillment of every prophecy regarding His birth. Truly ponder the depth of God's love for mankind to send His only, precious Son to die on the cross for our sins, ultimately changing our eternal destiny.

As you read the Christmas story, slow down and put yourself into the life of each character and each moment. Imagine what it would have felt like, what they went through, and how you may have reacted. Gather the family for nightly devotions covering slowly each part of the Christmas story, leading up to Christmas Day. Ask questions creating a family discussion. Don't just walk through the motions; make it count; let it change you.

This Christmas, take a step back from the busyness and prioritize time to ponder the reason we celebrate this special time of year. Don't wear yourself out and lose the joy of Christmas. Like Mary, ponder the wonder of His presence this season!

Ponder His Presence
Introduction by Hannah Kaspryzk

Merry Christmas!

Will You Accept the Greatest Gift?

By Marissa Patton

*For the wages of sin is death; but the gift of God
is eternal life through Jesus Christ our Lord.*

Romans 6:23

Christmas after Christmas rolls through the pages of my memory. Through the years, I have gotten many amazing gifts. One year, I received the whole collection of the Nancy Drew books. I thought I was in heaven! Another year, I got an MP3 player and headphones. Coolest kid around, I tell ya! As I grew older, I began to appreciate the practical gifts — a new sweater, a Christian marriage book, a nice set of kitchen utensils ... do not even get me started on the time my mom gifted me a new living room rug.

My point is, we all love receiving gifts. Especially ones that we can use on a day-to-day basis or have been in our Amazon cart for weeks. But I have to tell you about the greatest gift ever given to me — my salvation. Now, do not shut me out. If you have heard this story before, pretend like it is brand new. If you have already accepted this gift, keep reading. There is no way you cannot want to hear about the greatest gift that you have ever received.

Let's start at the beginning – Jesus' birth. I mean, that is why we celebrate Christmas. But why was He born into a sin-cursed world? Why would a perfect, heavenly Being like Christ want to come to earth? The answer: because He loved us. Okay ... so He loved us. Why did He have to come to Earth? Could He not just love us from heaven? Of course, He could! But He wanted us to have the opportunity to live a life free from sin! The only way that could be possible is for God to send His greatest Gift to us – Jesus – to die for us.

That is right. Jesus was born to die. There had to be a payment for our sin. That payment was the shed blood of a perfect Saviour. Jesus came to pay the punishment for our sins. Because, let's be honest, we have all sinned. "... For all have sinned, and come short of the glory of God;" Romans 3:23. Because of our sin, we could never have a relationship with a sinless God. We could never live a life free from the wickedness of ourselves. We could never feel the peace of Christ in our lives. Whoa! Sounds terribly sad and depressing, right?

I have good news: there is a gift. Jesus gave us a gift the day He died on the cross for us. His gift was salvation. His gift of salvation comes with so many benefits:

- Forgiveness for all sins — past, present, and future (Ephesians 1:7)

- Heavenly Father with limitless access through prayer (Hebrews 4:16)

- A Friend that will never leave or forsake us (Hebrews 13:5)

- The Holy Spirit to guide us (Romans 5:1-8)

- The peace of knowing He is taking care of us (Philippians 4:7)

Did I miss some? Probably. If you have taken this precious gift, remember the moment. Step back to the day you felt the peace of an almighty God. No earthly gift will ever compare. I remember the day I got saved. I was six years old. I remember walking out of the service after getting saved, determined to read my Bible all the way through. I was six. I did not meet that goal, as you can imagine. But the joy and zeal I had to learn about God and trust Him were so genuine in that childlike faith. Oh, that I would channel that joy and zeal in my adult life.

If you have never accepted that gift, you are missing out on the best decision you will ever make. Do not let this season go by without understanding the true gravity of Jesus' birth. He was born for you. He died for you. He longs to have a deep relationship with you. He wants to be your greatest gift. He is holding the gift out for you. Take it.

Admit that you are a sinner — "Wherefore, as by one man sin entered into the world, and death by sin; and so death passed upon all men, for that all have sinned:" Romans 5:12

Believe that Jesus died and rose again – "That if thou shalt confess with thy mouth the Lord Jesus, and shalt believe in thine heart that God hath raised him from the dead, thou shalt be saved." Romans 10:9.

Call on Him with a repentant heart – "For with the heart man believeth unto righteousness; and with the mouth confession is made unto salvation." Romans 10:10. "For whosoever shall call upon the name of the Lord shall be saved." Romans 10:13.

Let Him be the Hope of your heart – "Now the God of hope fill you with all joy and peace in believing, that ye may abound in hope, through the power of the Holy Ghost." Romans 15:13.

A THRILL OF

Hope

Verse

Devotion

Don't Let Christmas Festivities Become Weights

By Rikki Beth Poindexter

Wherefore seeing we also are compassed about with so great a cloud of witnesses, let us lay aside every weight, and the sin which doth so easily beset us, and let us run with patience the race that is set before us, Looking unto Jesus the author and finisher of our faith; who for the joy that was set before him endured the cross, despising the shame, and is set down at the right hand of the throne of God.

Hebrews 12:1-2

Weights are not sin — weights are things that distract or hinder and cause one to stand around or look back with regret.

The writer of Hebrews is saying we need to lay down the weights, the things that distract or hinder us, the things that may cause us to look back with regret. We are in a race but not a sprint, more like a marathon. We have to pace ourselves. This is a lesson that I have learned about Christmas festivities. We must keep our eyes on Jesus.

I have allowed the festivities of Christmas to become weights at the Most Wonderful Time of the Year! I have been distracted by events. I have regretted how I spent the month surrounding Christmas. My encouragement to you is, don't let Christmas activities become a weight. Keep our eyes on Jesus!

We know we should work hard to keep the main thing, the main thing.

The festivities of this time of the year are wonderful! I love all of the church festivities: the Sunday School parties, youth outings, and nursing home visits, Christmas games (I love games), play practices, and special services. I love all of the family and friend festivities you can get involved in around Christmas. I love to go look at lights, see holiday shows, invite people into our home, and visit others' homes. One can truly get overwhelmed (with the right kind of things) during this wonderful time of the year. Keep our eyes on Jesus!

As Christian women, we know that our hearts should be reflecting and centered on the birth of our Saviour at this time of the year, in particular. We have taught and trained our children in this way (or at least we should have). We know we should work hard to keep the main thing, the main thing. Many of us have made decisions on how we celebrate this time of the year to keep the Saviour at the forefront of our family's hearts and minds. We know what is right. Keep our eyes on Jesus!

I have found myself more times than I care to admit regretting that I had signed up for events, committed to an event, volunteered for events, or hosted events — good and right things. It simply was too much! Instead of enjoying the Most Wonderful Time of the Year, I was dreading the month of December and distracted by the "things." My commitments and plans had become a weight to me (not a sin). Sadly, my family paid the price for my overcommitment. I should have set some boundaries on what I would commit to or blocked off some days in my calendar. Keep our eyes on Jesus!

Be careful of what you sign up for or volunteer to do around the holidays. Leave days and weekends open for family time or simply nothing. Do not overcommit. It's okay to say "No" to a get-together or to a parade that is going to leave you exhausted afterward, or even angry that you committed to it before you even got there. Been there and done that! Keep our eyes on Jesus!

I do believe Christmas is the most wonderful time of the year! Our Saviour's birth deserves all the recognition and attention. It deserves celebrating, pondering, and reflecting. Be mindful that you do not overextend, overspend, or commit to too many extra things or events. Don't let the festivities of Christmas become weights. Keep our eyes on Jesus! Plan your Christmas calendar wisely.

Isaiah 9:6 "For unto us a child is born, unto us a son is given: and the government shall be upon his shoulder: and his name shall be called Wonderful, Counsellor, The mighty God, The everlasting Father, The Prince of Peace."

A THRILL OF

Hope

Verse

Devotion

A Shared Hope

By Bethany Riley

But sanctify the Lord God in your hearts: and be ready always to give an answer to every man that asketh you a reason of the hope that is in you with meekness and fear:

I Peter 3:15

I am so thankful for the hope that is in me. I'm so thankful that Jesus Christ is my hope of eternal life. It's only through Him that we have salvation, and it's only because of Him that we have any hope at all. (Romans 5:1-2, Romans 15:10-13). The focus of Christmas should be the Gift wrapped in swaddling clothes that God gave to us. He is the "reason for the hope that is in you." But being thankful isn't enough; I must be ready to give an answer to every man that asketh.

We live in a world filled with hopeless people. Some may be spending time with family, hosting Christmas parties, and running around to all the events that make this time of year so special. Some may have to celebrate this time of year alone. Regardless of their circumstances, if they are lost, they are hopeless. People around us are searching for something, trying to find just a glimpse of hope. They are weary.

Am I telling those around me about what Jesus did for me?

They pass right by the nativity scenes and Christmas plays, not knowing that what they need is right in front of them. But Romans 10:14 asks, "How then shall they call on him in whom they have not believed? and how shall they believe in him of whom they have not heard? and how shall they hear without a preacher?" We are called to be "a preacher" (defined as a herald, public crier). We have exactly what they are looking for dwelling inside of us. They need God's precious Son!

Am I telling those around me about what Jesus did for me? Am I telling others how wonderful He is, why I can have peace and joy? Am I living a life that would cause someone to ask me about my hope? Or am I acting and looking like just another lost sinner? Before you are ready to give an answer, you must "sanctify the Lord God in your hearts" first. "Sanctify" in this verse means "to make holy; ceremonially purify or consecrate."

I am guilty of being so caught up in the fun of the season that I forget to share the Gospel, when really that should be the focus of my everyday life (Romans 10:9-15). I want this Christmas season to be different. The young girl (yes, with the nose rings, tattoos, and purple hair) who's making my coffee needs the hope that I carry around with me. The homeless man (yes, a bit sketchy) I see at the same place on the way to work every day needs that hope that I have! And yes, even the mom at the kid's function, who seems to have it all together but is really dead inside and on the way to an eternity without God, needs the hope of eternal life that I so freely possess. Maybe all I have time for is a tract and a smile; maybe I can get a kind word and an invitation to church. Remember, we are to answer with meekness and fear.

Whatever opportunities the Lord may give me this Christmas season to share "the reason of the hope that is in you", I want to seize them! Too often, I let those moments slip right by me. One of my favorite lines of my all-time favorite Christmas carol is "A thrill of hope, the weary world rejoices, for yonder breaks a new and glorious morn!" What a thrill of hope we've been given in the birth of Jesus Christ! What am I doing to share it with a weary world?

Hope

Verse

Devotion

God With Us

By Victoria Kiker

Behold, a virgin shall be with child, and shall bring forth a son,
and they shall call his name Emmanuel, which being interpreted is, God with us.

Matthew 1:23

Let's take a trip with our imagination to the home of a young girl named Mary as she eagerly awaits her marriage to her betrothed, Joseph, a just and quiet man. One ordinary day, Mary was suddenly interrupted by Gabriel, an angel of God, who had come to deliver an important and world-changing message to her. The Holy Ghost of God would come upon her, overshadow her, and place in her womb "that holy thing" (Luke 1:35) which should be called the Son of God. How could this be? Mary, in her virginity, had not known a man. Her mind was whirling; this could very well be the end of her betrothal to Joseph. Would he understand? Would her family or friends believe her? Her life may very well be at stake, but with faith, Mary humbly said,

"Behold, the handmaid of the Lord; be it unto me according to thy word..."(Luke 1:38).

Mary did not know what the future held, but even in the loneliness and isolation, she believed.

I wonder if Mary felt turmoil and fear crowd her heart as she perhaps wrestled with the extraordinary news that had been given her. Even more than that, I wonder if Mary felt alone and isolated even though she was carrying the most precious gift given to not only her, but the world. Within her very womb, Emmanuel (God with us) was developing and growing to one day become her Saviour. Mary did not know what the future held for her or for her growing Son, but she believed. Even in the loneliness and isolation, she believed.

Christmas is a wondrous time of year; a time of family and friends, of gifts and parties, of decorating and cookie baking. The nostalgic memories that take you back to childhood and years gone by can be beautiful moments of reflection. But for some, Christmas can be an extremely lonely and depressing time. For you, dear sister, I am writing.

The "most wonderful time of the year" may feel heavy for you. You may have one less place setting around your table this year due to a loss; you may be missing family and friends who live far away. You may have just entered the empty nesting stage and are missing your children deeply, or you may be in the throes of caring for young children or aging parents, and the very thought of making "special memories" or a Pinterest-perfect home for Christmas feels like just "one more thing" to add onto your very full plate. I understand! I've spent a few Christmas seasons just wishing the time away.

It's within these times that you and I need to remind ourselves of the nearness of Emmanuel. GOD IS WITH YOU! He is with you in the places that are lonely, isolated, and difficult to bear. He is with you at your empty table. He is with you across the world, in another state, another country. He is with you in grief. He is with you in your chaos. Allow Jesus to be your Emmanuel this Christmas season. Ask Him to be with you and near you in the difficult moments. In your times of prayer, just sit and meditate on the fact that He is with you. The very thought should simultaneously humble and thrill us. What a precious God we have! Knowing that He left Heaven in all its glory and splendor and chose to be with me is astonishing!

My prayer for you during this holiday season is that you would experience the closeness of Emmanuel. May Emmanuel fill all the empty places in your heart and home, reminding you of how much you are loved and known by Him. Don't forget, He is in you and with you! Merry Christmas from my heart to yours!

A THRILL OF

Hope

Verse

Devotion

When Faith Is Quiet:
The Pondering of Mary

By Lauren Speares

But Mary kept all these things, and pondered them in her heart.

Luke 2:19

When reading the Christmas story, the one verse that always stuck out to me is Luke 2:19. I find this interesting because in the verses leading up to verse 19, everyone is praising the Lord and worshipping. Still, you get to Mary, and she is pondering. So the question I ask is, why was Mary pondering when the world around her was praising? To find the answer, I believe we have to go back to before the birth of Christ.

Mary was a pure, faithful young lady who had a desire to please the Lord. At this point in her life, she is engaged to Joseph, a just man (Matthew 1:19), who also had a desire to please and serve the Lord. I imagine that Mary is excited about this time in her life. Then an angel appears before Mary and informs her that she will

Keep trusting and believing in God who keeps His promises.

be the mother of Jesus. Mary tells the angel, "How shall this be, seeing I know not a man?" (Luke 1:34). The angel reminds her of her cousin Elisabeth, who conceived in her old age, and that with God, nothing is impossible (Luke 1:35-37).

I can only imagine the thoughts going through Mary's mind. Mary was willing to do this because she was a servant of the Lord (Luke 1:38). Mary did not ask the angel for a sign; she just believed and trusted that God would fulfill the promise she was given. Elisabeth affirms this for her by saying, "And blessed is she that believed; for there shall be a performance of those things which were told her from the Lord." (Luke 1:45).

Mary begins to magnify the Lord and worship him! Mary knows that God has made this promise, and He is going to keep it. Mary begins thanking God in awe, who would even have anything to do with her (Luke 1:46-55). She recognizes that God is faithful and will not fail her!

The Bible only gives us a little under two chapters to cover the entire nine months of Mary's pregnancy, so I can't say for sure how this time in her life went, but I certainly can imagine. She was most likely belittled, mocked, and berated on top of all the natural discomfort of pregnancy. I'm sure she lost friends during this time, and we know she almost lost her groom, Joseph (Matthew 1:19). Again, I cannot say for sure, but I believe that Mary's worship was short-term. Mary was just as much flesh as we are, and probably let the circumstances around her dim her praise.

I believe this is what happened for the wise men, shepherds, and all those who were told Jesus had been born. They were thrilled that the Son of God had been born in a lowly manger! Although we don't know what happened to these men and women after the birth of Christ, you cannot find in the Bible where they were still worshipping after it. Were they doubting that Jesus truly was the Son of God, or did they forget that God had fulfilled his promise?

However, Mary was found to be pondering the night Jesus was born. I believe at this moment, Mary is holding baby Jesus, looking at His precious face, pondering on the fact that the promise God had given her had been fulfilled. What Mary was doing was not short-term; it was long-term. She knew deep in her heart that God is real, faithful to His promises, and she would never have to question otherwise. This is why you can find Mary at the wedding of Cana, telling the servants to do what Jesus said, because she knew He had a purpose, and it would be fulfilled (John 2:3).

Friend, there will be times when God gives you a promise, and it is hard to keep praising him in your circumstances. Keep trusting and believing in God, who keeps His promises and is faithful to fulfill them! Not only that, but don't forget about what He has done. Ponder on those fulfilled promises!

A THRILL OF

Hope

Verse

Devotion

My Gift To Him

By Hannah Suttle

O give thanks unto the LORD, for he is good: for his mercy endureth for ever.

Psalm 107:1

David is one character in the Bible that we all know well. His testimony of having a heart for God started at a young age when he, the smallest of all his brothers, fought and defeated the giant Goliath. In his own strength, this was impossible, but he put His trust in God to win this battle. (1 Samuel 17) He found a friend in Jonathan, the son of the king, whose greatest desire was to kill him. But still, he put His trust in God for the victory over this trial, and praised the Lord for deliverance from those who wished him evil. (2 Samuel 22, Psalm 18) When David became king, he won battles for Israel and developed a reputation for being a strong king, but even then, David was not perfect. He made a mistake, and the consequences affected the rest of his life and his family. He desired to build a temple to honor the Lord, but because of his sin, the Lord would not allow it. Even then, David offered the Lord his worship and praise with a grateful heart for the Lord's tender care and mercies. (2 Samuel 7:18-29, 1 Chronicles 17:16-27)

37

David did not allow the tragedies in his life to define how he worshiped the Lord; he didn't become bitter and question why God allowed these things to happen. Rather, he allowed the circumstances to draw him closer to the Lord and increase his praise in awe of God's goodness. In fact, Psalm 119:164 says that David praised the Lord seven times a day!

In review of David's life and relationship with the Lord, I want to give the Lord the greatest gift I can – a dedicated life, my trust, and my praise! He deserves all of the glory. God may not answer my prayers the way I wanted, but His way is always better. He deserves the gift of my trust and praise that He is guiding my life in a purpose beyond my imagination. He deserves my gratitude for the victory over struggles and trials, before He even delivers me from them. So ask yourself, what can I give God today to bring Him honor and glory with the life He has blessed me with?

A THRILL OF

Hope

Verse

Devotion

Hope Was Born

By Grace Shiflett

For unto you is born this day in the city of David a Saviour, which is Christ the Lord.

Luke 2:11

The Christmas season is such a beautiful time to pause and ponder Jesus. We often say with our lips, "It's all about Him!"—but is it really?

It's so easy to get caught up in the hustle and bustle and lose sight of the true meaning. I don't think it's intentional — we don't set out to do this — but so often we end up stressing over things that don't matter. When that happens, we don't even enjoy the season the way we should. Honestly, it would be better to go without the decorations, leave that shopping list unfinished, or skip the baking if those things pull us away from the meaning of Christmas.

It's sad when the world shapes us to fix our eyes on all the fluff of the season, and in doing so, we miss the moments that matter most. When we get swept up in commercialism, we fail ourselves, our families, and even the lost world that needs to see Christ.

For me, Christmas is like a spiritual reset as the new year approaches. I go back to the manger, then follow the story to the cross, on to the empty tomb, and finally to that blessed hope of His return! It all started in a lowly stable – Hope was born! Jesus came so we could have life and have it more abundantly. He was born to die, yes, but He was also born to live. After three days in the tomb, He rose again – victorious over death, Hell, and the grave.

This season, let's encourage one another not to get lost in the "spirit" of Christmas and miss the reason for the season. If you've received the free gift of salvation, you carry that hope with you not only in December but throughout the year.

Let the story of Christ's coming refresh you this season – and every season that follows.

As children of God, we live in anticipation of that blessed hope: the promise that Jesus will come again. But this time, He will not come as a babe in a manger – He will return as King of Kings and Lord of Lords. He is coming back for His own. Are you ready? Are you waiting with a thrill of hope?

"Looking for that blessed hope, and the glorious appearing of the great God and our Saviour Jesus Christ;" (Titus 2:13)

May every celebration this Christmas draw us closer to the true reason for the season – Jesus.

A THRILL OF

Hope

Verse

Devotion

He Wants You!

By Alicia Moss

Furthermore David the king said unto all the congregation, Solomon my son, whom alone God hath chosen, is yet young and tender, and the work is great: for the palace is not for man, but for the LORD God.

1 Chronicles 29:1

'Tis the season to be jolly ... "C is for the Christ child who died for us" ... "Angels we have heard on high" ... "Mary, did you know" ... "Joy to the World the Lord is Come" ... Are you singing yet? When I think of Christmas, I sing, I decorate, and I create my Christmas cards to mail off. Those are the things I love doing around the Christmas season. I love the beautiful lights while listening to my favorite Christmas songs. I love addressing envelopes and going to the mailbox to see the Christmas pictures or handwritten Christmas greetings from across the states. However, as much as I love this season, I do not enjoy the pressure of gift-giving and the desire to do more than is practical. The older my children become, the more I wonder if I'm making all the memories possible. Will they look back and say Christmas was wonderful when we were kids?

45

Don't choose to tell Him, "No." Tell Him, "Yes!"

I wonder how Mary felt that first Christmas. What were her worries? What were her fears? I have no doubt she was excited, as most new mothers are. I have no doubt she was anxious about the birthing place and the culture surrounding her. BUT she was delivering the Son of God! Yes, she was probably in awe of Him, but oh, the fear of knowing she was the mother of the Son of God!

While reading 1 Chronicles 29:1, the Lord reminded me of Mary. "Furthermore David the king said unto all the congregation, Solomon my son, whom alone God hath chosen, is yet young and tender, and the work is great: for the palace is not for man, but for the Lord God." God chose Mary to be the earthly mother of Jesus just as he chose Solomon to be king. Mary was young and tender, just as Solomon was young and tender. The Bible states that Solomon's work was great, just as the job the Lord had given Mary was great. The job Solomon was given to accomplish was not for man but for the Lord. Although Jesus was Mary's earthly Son, He was not for her. He was to fulfill the purpose of the Lord God.

Are you young and tender physically? The Lord wants You! Are you young and tender spiritually? The Lord wants you. The second part of II Peter 3:9 states that the Lord is "not willing that any should perish, but that all should come to repentance." The Lord wants to save you this Christmas season. He came to this world through the womb of Mary to die on the cross and save you! He also wants to give to you.

One of His attributes is goodness. The Psalmist said, "The Lord is good." Allow Him to be good to you. Don't shame Him; allow Him to give all the good He's got for you.

Solomon's work was great. Mary's work was great. The work God has for you is great, too! Are you meeting the potential God has for your life? Are you diligently seeking to make yourself better for his glory? Are you actively reading His Word, ready to serve? What is an area the Lord has dealt with you about but you've chosen to ignore? You've chosen to say, "No, Lord, I'm not ready to work on that area of my life." Don't choose to tell Him,"No." Tell Him "Yes!" Try! The work is great, allow Him to use your life.

Lastly, Solomon worked for the Lord. Mary's work was done for the Lord. Remember, your purpose is for the Lord. Whatever you do this Christmas season, do it for the Lord. Colossians 3:23-24 "And whatsoever ye do, do it heartily, as to the Lord, and not unto men; Knowing that of the Lord ye shall receive the reward of the inheritance: for ye serve the Lord Christ." While I address the envelopes to my Christmas cards, I need to do it to the Lord. As I decorate for the Christmas season, I need to do it thoughtfully and unto the Lord. Maybe this Christmas season, I need to stop some traditions if they are hindering me from my purpose to the Lord. We have one earthly life to live. Live your life for the Lord! He only wants you!

A THRILL OF

Hope

Verse

Devotion

Snow Globes

By Kelly Byrley

For I know the thoughts that I think toward you, saith the LORD,
thoughts of peace, and not of evil, to give you an expected end.

Jeremiah 29:11

Do you enjoy snow globes? I sure do. I love taking in all the details of the peaceful scene that's on the inside and then giving it a good shake so I can watch the beautiful snow fall all around.

Our lives can be like a snow globe. We can be at ease, and then suddenly, the Lord comes along and gives our peaceful little world a good shake. We are thrown off balance for a minute during the chaos. If we aren't clinging to something solid and strong, we fall and become injured. The things around us that aren't secure begin to fall and break. We may be scared, angry, confused, frustrated, sad, or experience many other negative emotions. Happy, excited, grateful, and other positive emotions are usually not the emotions we feel ... at least during the shaking. It may feel like the shaking will never end, but it does. When it stops, we immediately begin looking around to survey the damage. We see that some of our things are broken and destroyed.

If we are honest with ourselves, some of these things were just clutter or distractions that we should've gotten rid of a long time ago. They are things that were taking up the space we should have made available for more important things. However, scattered among all this rubble, we sadly realize that not all the things that are broken were unnecessary. Some of them were truly precious to us. We are heartbroken as we realize they are now damaged or destroyed. We are filled with regret because we never took the time or energy to properly secure them, despite knowing that we should. After the initial shock begins to wear off, we start to inspect ourselves. We may be hurt or injured, but how badly is determined by what we were clinging to when the shaking started. If we were clinging to something that wasn't secure enough to withstand the disruption or if we were relying on our own balance to keep us steady, our injuries would be greater. If we were clinging to something steadfast, we might have minor injuries or even escaped the ordeal mostly unharmed.

During all of this, the snow has started to fall, and people have gathered around to watch. They are automatically drawn to the scene to watch the beautiful snowfall. They see us inside as we start to clean up our mess and heal from our injuries. They see us as we discard the unnecessary things that were cluttering up our lives. They see us as we repair the precious things and do our best to secure them from future damage. They see us heal and become stronger. Hopefully, they see us make better spiritual choices. They watch as we nail down the solid, unwavering thing we will cling to when the next jolt comes. They also watch as, throughout this rebuilding and healing process, we also take the time to enjoy the beauty of the falling snow. As the snow blankets the area, we feel the sweet peace and stillness that uniquely comes after a fresh snowfall. Then we understand that without the shaking, there can be no snow.

You might wonder why I chose Jeremiah 29:11 as my main verse since it doesn't have anything to do with snow globes, which has been the theme of this devotional. I chose it because it has to do with how God feels about us. The shaking He does in our lives is not to harm us, but rather to purge us, strengthen us, change us, and allow us to be a better example for others. He has an expected path with an expected end for each of us, and sometimes our lives need to be shaken up a bit to keep us on that path. Let's ask ourselves a few questions.

What do I need to discard in my life that is cluttering up my time and energy?

- "Wherefore seeing we also are compassed about with so great a cloud of witnesses, let us lay aside every weight, and the sin which doth so easily beset us, and let us run with patience the race that is set before us," Hebrews 12:1

- "And that which fell among thorns are they, which, when they have heard, go forth, and are choked with cares and riches and pleasures of this life, and bring no fruit to perfection." Luke 8:14

What precious things do I need to protect and secure in my heart and life?

- "Keep thy heart with all diligence; for out of it are the issues of life." Proverbs 4:23

- "For they that are after the flesh do mind the things of the flesh; but they that are after the Spirit the things of the Spirit." Romans 8:5

What sort of support do I cling to when the shaking starts?

- "The LORD is my rock, and my fortress, and my deliverer; my God, my strength, in whom I will trust; my buckler, and the horn of my salvation, and my high tower." Psalm 18:2

- "Fear thou not; for I am with thee: be not dismayed; for I am thy God: I will strengthen thee; yea, I will help thee; yea, I will uphold thee with the right hand of my righteousness." Isaiah 41:10

Since the Lord gave me this thought over a year ago, I have been reminded of these things every time I have seen a snow globe, and I pray that this would also be true for you.

Hope

Verse

Devotion

Pausing to Ponder

By Larissa Bell

But Mary kept all these things, and pondered them in her heart.

Luke 2:19

Have you ever had a situation or season of life that was so overwhelming or challenging that it made you need to step back and wonder what God was doing? Even in good times, life seems to come at you so fast you feel like a toddler trying to drink from a gushing garden hose. I wonder if that is how Mary was feeling after giving birth to the Son of God in a stable with a bunch of strangers barging into her borrowed stall, explaining that angels singing in the sky told them where the Baby was! But she pondered.

According to the 1828 Webster's dictionary, to ponder means "to weigh in the mind; to consider and compare the circumstances or consequences of an event." Mary, the mother of Jesus, had a lot to ponder!

Pondering the Past

For hundreds of years, her people had been oppressed and not heard from God as they once did from the prophets. Yet, in the middle of an ordinary life on a previously ordinary day, she also had an angel visit her. He told her she was the virgin chosen to bear the Son of God, the promised Messiah! Maybe she remembered visiting her cousin, Elizabeth, when the unborn John the Baptist leaped for joy when Jesus entered the room (Luke 1:44). Mary also may have been thinking about the journey that brought Joseph and her to Bethlehem — seemingly for tax reasons — but we know it was ultimately God providing a way to fulfill Micah 5:2 that foretold of the Saviour being born in Bethlehem, an unassuming town "among the thousands of Judah." These events that she recalled were fingerprints of the Almighty in her life; they confirmed the promises of God and bolstered her faith. Take some time to ponder the fingerprints along your journey that confirm God is working in your life. "I remember the days of old; I meditate on all thy works; I muse on the work of thy hands" (Psalm 143:5).

Pondering the Present

Can you imagine what was going through Mary's mind as she gazed into the face of Jesus? He was just a tiny baby in her arms, but a mighty King of Kings in Heaven. Did she dream about what He would look like and what talents He would have? Could she have known He would heal the sick and make food for one lunch stretch into twelve baskets of leftovers? Was she wondering how she would help raise Jesus and train Him in the way He should go so He could fulfill all the Scriptures and His purpose for being born?

I have pondered – okay, I have worried – many times that my imperfect flesh may "mess up" what God has planned for my children and others in my church family who look up to me. We know God helped Mary, and He can still help us today as mothers, grandmothers, aunts, sisters, friends, and church ministry workers to positively influence those around us to seek and pursue God's will for their lives. Ponder ways God has helped you minister to your family and those around you. Thank Him for His wisdom, guidance, and patience with you, and extend it to those precious gifts in your life! (Phil 1:6)

Pondering the Future

A thought that makes me sad when I read the verse about Mary pondering these things in her heart is knowing that this little Baby she held was born to die on Calvary. I don't know exactly what Mary grasped at that point in her life about the future suffering of Jesus, but she likely would have heard the passage from Isaiah about Him being "wounded for our transgressions" and "with His stripes we are healed."

No mother wants to think about their baby being rejected by people or dying a painful death, but that may have weighed heavily on her heart as the worship from the shepherds confirmed that Jesus was the perfect Lamb of God. It hurt God's heart, too, to send His only Son to die for the sins of the world and to have to turn His back on Jesus when He carried those sins on the cross. But He did it for whosoever will believe on Him (2 Peter 3:9). If you have never accepted this precious gift of salvation, what better time than right now? Ponder your Spiritual condition and surrender to God's direction for your future. Commit your way to Him, trust Him, and praise Him for what He will do through you in the future! (Ps 37:5)

Hope

Verse

Devotion

Not Without Hope

By Misty Wells

But I would not have you to be ignorant, brethren, concerning them which are asleep, that ye sorrow not, even as those which have no hope.

I Thessalonians 4:13

It's the third day of going through my grandmother's earthly possessions. Room by room, we have opened and swept through closets and dressers. Her Bibles and books have been divided among the family, and the smallest note or word written by her will be treasured always. Little boxes of "bits and bobs" are pulled out, and we can somewhat chuckle as we reminisce about the fact that Grandma hesitated to throw anything away. Most of her collections had a potential purpose or some sentimental value that meant something to her. Beautiful handmade crochet blankets and scarves are admired and distributed among those who value such things. As the last Christmas mug is placed into a box, the reality that she will never use her things again begins to set in. Our hearts are broken, and we find ourselves grieving even as others who have no hope.

"Looking for that blessed hope, and the glorious appearing of the great God and our Saviour Jesus Christ;"

- Titus 2:13

We are not the only ones who have felt hopeless. Before Christ's birth, the Jewish people longed for their Messiah. Isaiah 7:14 tells us that He would be born of a virgin. Micah 5:12 foretells his birth in Bethlehem. Isaiah 9:6 describes their coming King as a "Wonderful, Counselor, The Mighty God, The Everlasting Father, and The Prince of Peace." They knew He was coming, but many would die never having seen their long-awaited Saviour. Wives would bury their husbands. Many children would say goodbye to their parents. The loss of loved ones would be grieved time and time again before Christ's coming. Would the Wonderful Counselor ever make his appearance? Would the Prince of Peace ever bring Peace to those who had waited so long?

In I Thessalonians, we find another people waiting for the return of Christ, and in their waiting, they are grieving the loss of family. What would happen to those who are asleep in Christ? Paul says, "But I would not have you to be ignorant, brethren concerning them which are asleep, that ye sorrow not, even as others which have no hope." I Thessalonians 4:13. He says, "For the Lord Himself shall descend from Heaven with a shout, with the voice of the archangel, and with the trump of God: and the dead in Christ shall rise first. Then we, who are alive and remain, shall be caught up together with them in the clouds, to meet the Lord in the air: and so shall we ever be with the Lord." I Thessalonians 4:16-17.

Death, even for those who have trusted Jesus as their Saviour, brings sorrow, but we are not without hope. The Messiah did come just as the prophets predicted. He was born of a virgin in the little town of Bethlehem. He lived a sinless life and on the cross of Calvary, He shed His precious blood to pay the ultimate price for our sins. Yes, He did come then, and He will come again to take His children home. My prayer is that your heart will be comforted with the hope of His glorious return (I Thess 4:18) ... And so shall we ever be with the Lord.

"Now the God of hope fill you with all joy and peace in believing, that ye may abound in hope, through the power of the Holy Ghost." Romans 15:13

"Looking for that blessed hope, and the glorious appearing of the great God and our Saviour Jesus Christ;" Titus 2:13

A THRILL OF

Hope

Verse

Devotion

The Christ of the Cradle

By Anja Meyer

And they came with haste, and found Mary, and Joseph, and the babe lying in a manger.

Luke 2:16

There is truly nothing like the spectacular lights, cozy decorations, and festive foods around Christmastime. However, when I look around our society, I realize that the celebrations are about everything except Christ. Therefore, I would like us to take a moment to celebrate, worship, and just stand in awe of our wonderful Christ who came to a cradle.

This baby was and is God. He is not a man who became God, but God Who became a man.

"In the beginning was the Word, and the Word was with God, and the Word was God. And the Word was made flesh, and dwelt among us," John 1:1, 14a

The long-awaited Messiah finally arrived there in Bethlehem! There are upwards of 300 prophecies from the Old Testament that are fulfilled in the Lord Jesus.

"...We have found the Messias, which is, being interpreted, the Christ." John 1:41b

This Man was born to be the King of Israel. Through both the natural line of Mary (Luke 3) and the adopted royal line of Joseph (Matthew 1), Jesus was to sit on the throne of Israel. "Rabbi, thou art the Son of God; thou art the King of Israel." John 1:49

Christ, Who came in a cradle, is Master and Lord. He is the One Who issues commands. He is the One Who should be obeyed. "Ye call me Master and Lord: and ye say well; for so I am." John 13:13

Christ is also our Saviour. He is the Door through which we enter to be saved. There is no other means of getting rid of our sins and getting right with God. "I am the door: by me if any man enter in, he shall be saved, and shall go in and out, and find pasture." John 10:9

Christ is the Way, the Truth, and the Life. When we get confused with different ideas and do not know where to go or what to do, we turn to our loving Saviour. Only in Him do we reach the Father. "Jesus saith unto him, I am the way, the truth, and the life: no man cometh unto the Father, but by me." John 14:6

Our Saviour is our good Shepherd. He does not leave us to our own devices or abandon us when things go wrong. He leads us to green pastures and still waters. "I am the good shepherd: the good shepherd giveth his life for the sheep." John 10:11

Christ is our Bread. He is the Saviour Who at once gave us everlasting life, and He is the Word Who feeds us daily. "I am that bread of life." John 6:48

Christ is the true Vine. Only when we abide in Him can we bear fruit to glorify Him and bless others around us. Our own efforts are as filthy rags. "I am the vine, ye are the branches: He that abideth in me, and I in him, the same bringeth forth much fruit: for without me ye can do nothing." John 15:5

Christ is our Light. In this ever-darkening world, we need Light more and more for guidance and safety. "In him was life; and the life was the light of men." John 1:4

Christ is the Resurrection. What a wonderful hope to have, that we will be resurrected to be with Him forever! This world is not our home; we're just passing through. "Jesus said unto her, I am the resurrection, and the life: he that believeth in me, though he were dead, yet shall he live:" John 11:25

Our Saviour is our Example. We are not in the dark about what is expected of us. We can follow in His footsteps. "For I have given you an example, that ye should do as I have done to you." John 13:15 (See also Philippians 2:5 and Colossians 3:13)

Christ is all of these wonderful things, but He poses this question, "But whom say ye that I am?" (Matthew 16:15). Each of us needs to answer that vitally important question for ourselves as soon as possible.

When a person first gets saved, she might not immediately understand everything, but there will be no doubt in her mind that she has had a life-changing encounter with the living God. This was the reply of the blind man whose eyes were opened by the Lord Jesus Christ, when he was pressured and threatened by the Jews: "Whether he be a sinner or no, I know not: one thing I know, that, whereas I was blind, now I see." (John 9:25)

When Christ saves your soul, you enter into a sweet relationship with Him. You commune with Him, enjoy His presence, and see Him work in your life. Even in your deepest distress, you recognize His voice and trust Him when He says, "It is I; be not afraid." (John 6:20)

Do take the time to commit the Gospel of John to memory. You will be greatly blessed thereby!

A THRILL OF

Hope

Verse

Devotion

Three Treasures of Wise Women

By Courtney Womack

...We have seen his star in the east, and are come to worship him.

Matthew 2:2b

When we think of Christmas, certain images come to mind: the smell of freshly baked cookies, family gatherings, the rush of shopping and wrapping gifts in vibrant-colored paper, picking out the perfect outfit for the Christmas church service, or watching snow gently fall outside while sipping a warm drink by the fire.

These are all beautiful parts of the season, but they are far removed from the very first Christmas. Today, I want us to shift our mindset. Let's step away from the modern version of Christmas and imagine what it was like for those who lived in anticipation of a Saviour. They held on to promises passed down through generations, stories of a coming King, a Redeemer, a bringer of peace. But at the time, it was just that: a promise, a hope, not yet fulfilled.

Now, let's focus on a group of individuals often misrepresented or misunderstood: the Wisemen. These men weren't just casual travelers. They were scholars, students of prophecy, science, and the stars. They had studied the ancient Scriptures, listened to the stories handed down, and earnestly sought the Messiah. Their journey wasn't quick or convenient. Yet they made it, because they were determined to find the Saviour.

Like the wisemen, we too are called to seek Him, not just during Christmas, but daily. In the midst of our hectic lives filled with shopping, to-do lists, ministry obligations, and meals to prepare, how often do we pause and ask: Lord, what would You have me do in this moment?

Seek Him with Purpose

The wisemen sought Jesus with purpose. They didn't just stumble upon Him. Their pursuit was long, and it required patience, study, and faith. During the holiday season, it's easy to lose sight of this. The noise of the world can drown out our spiritual focus. But Jeremiah 29:13 reminds us, "and ye shall seek me, and find me, when ye shall search for me with all your heart."

Don't let the busyness of the season steal your time with the Saviour. Quiet your heart. Listen for His voice. Seek Him and His will on purpose.

Settle Your Heart on Truth

In Matthew 2, we read how the wise men stopped in Jerusalem and encountered Herod. Though he pretended to care, Herod was deceitful and jealous. But God warned the wise men not to return to him, and they obeyed. In doing so, they protected Jesus and were blessed with the opportunity to worship Him.

Today, we too are bombarded with messages that pull us away from the truth. Lies about our worth, distractions from God's purpose, spiritual confusion wrapped in pretty packaging. But just like the wise men, we must cling to God's Word.

Settle your heart. Turn down the volume of the world. Refuse to let the enemy distract you from the Truth.

Serve Him with Your Gifts

Matthew 2:11 tells us the wise men brought gifts: gold, frankincense, and myrrh. These were not random tokens. Each carried deep meaning, and each has something to teach us about how we, too, can offer ourselves to Jesus.

- Gold: A symbol of value and kingship. Isaiah 43:4 says that we are precious in God's sight. The greatest gift you can give Jesus is your heart. He came to give His life for yours. What better way to honor Him than to surrender your life in return?

- Frankincense: A costly incense used in worship (Exodus 30). This reminds us to give Jesus our worship, not just our hearts, but our full devotion. To worship is to elevate Him above all else in your life. It's choosing His will over your own.

- Myrrh: A burial spice, used in times of pain, grief, and purification. This symbolizes our suffering and surrender. Even in seasons of bitterness or loss, we are called to trust in God's plan and offer Him our grief as faith and loving submission.

As we celebrate Christmas this year, let's not lose sight of the true gift: Jesus Himself. He came not in grandeur, but in humility. Not as a warrior king, but as a baby in a manger. He is the greatest gift, and He is still worthy of our pursuit, our truth, and our treasures.

A THRILL OF

Hope

Verse

Devotion

"And You Spell It O-B-E-D-I-E-N-C-E"

By Cristy Tadlock

And Mary said, Behold the handmaid of the Lord; be it unto me according to thy word. And the angel departed from her.

Luke 1:38

The Christmas Story is one of my favorite events in the Bible. It's such a beautiful example of God's love and sacrifice. The world had abided in years of silence from God between the Old and New Testaments, then suddenly the stage was set for the brightest light of all, Jesus. Who is your favorite character? What portion would you have liked to have been a "fly on the wall" for? One character trait that is obvious in all the characters in the Christmas Story is their obedience to God.

First, look at Mary (Luke 1). When the angel came to her and declared to her what was fixing to happen, she was obviously scared (verse 29). But she listened, she trusted, and she obeyed. In her humanity, she knew it was impossible, but her spirit knew that with God,

Obedience to Him is always the correct response.

all things are possible. "And Mary said, Behold the handmaid of the Lord; be it unto me according to thy word. And the angel departed from her." Luke 1:38

Next, look at Joseph. I can't imagine what was going through his mind when he found out Mary, his Mary, was expecting a child (Matthew 1). The angel came to him in a dream and told him to fear not and to continue as planned to make Mary his wife. The angel even told Joseph what the baby's name would be, Jesus (verse 21)! Joseph obeyed God and became the earthly father of God's only begotten Son, Jesus. "Then Joseph being raised from sleep did as the angel of the Lord had hidden him, and took unto him his wife:" Matthew 1:24

Thirdly, look at the shepherds. Just a group of innocent bystanders who were out doing their work one night when suddenly a host of angels burst on the scene with the amazing news of Jesus' birth (Luke 2). The angel of the Lord told the shepherds where to find Jesus, and they immediately decided to go and worship. "And it came to pass, as the angels were gone away from them into heaven, the shepherds said one to another, Let us now go even unto Bethlehem, and see this thing which is come to pass, which the Lord hath made known unto us." Luke 2:15

Lastly, the obedience of the wise men (Matthew 2). They journeyed from the East searching for the King of the Jews. We know King Herod felt threatened by the new king in town and told the wise men to report back to him after they found Jesus. But after finding Jesus, worshipping, and presenting their gifts, God told them not to report back to Herod. They listened in obedience and returned to their countries another way. "And being warned of God in a dream that they should not return to Herod, they departed into their own country another way." Matthew 2:12

In conclusion, what do all these characters have in common? Obedience. It really is the very best way to show God and others that you believe. Are you in obedience to His call? His commands? Regardless of where you are in the story, God is writing your life. Obedience to Him is always the correct response.

A THRILL OF

Hope

Verse

Devotion

When God Has Another Plan

By Hannah Kaspryzk

Now the birth of Jesus Christ was on this wise: When as his mother Mary was espoused to Joseph, before they came together, she was found with child of the Holy Ghost.

Matthew 1:18

Mary and Joseph were two pure, godly young people preparing and anticipating the day they would be married. I'm sure they were full of dreams and plans for how their life together would be! Before they even made it to the wedding, God flipped their world upside down when He chose them to raise His Son, Jesus. Mary and Joseph were each faced with a choice – would they obey God's plan or cling to their own? Thankfully, Mary and Joseph each had separate moments in which they surrendered to God.

Mary's surrender is seen in Luke 1:38a, "And Mary said, Behold the handmaid of the Lord; be it unto me according to thy word." Joseph's surrender is found in Matthew 1:24, "Then Joseph being raised from sleep did as the angel of the Lord had bidden him, and took unto him his wife:" God directed their lives again when they were forced to travel to Bethlehem for the census, and Jesus was born. Later, after the wise men's visit, God told them to flee to Egypt. Just when they felt they would always live in Egypt, God relocated them to Nazareth. This much traveling and uprooting was not in Mary and Joseph's plans for their life, but it was all in God's perfect plan.

God directs each of our lives, guiding us step by step into His perfect will. Sometimes God's plan looks very different than how we expected. The promises in Scripture remind us that God's ways are best. Psalm 18:30 and 32 says, "As for God, his way is perfect: the will of the Lord is tried: he is a buckler to all those that trust in Him. It is God that girdeth me with strength, and maketh my way perfect." Will you trust and obey God when it changes the direction of your life? We never know when God is going to lead us to the next step of His plan, so it is essential that we remain surrendered.

When Mary and Joseph surrendered their lives to obey God's plan, they endured the skepticism and side glances from those around them. The community probably gossiped about the situation and despised Mary and Joseph, not understanding the miracle of fulfilled prophecy that happened. The world around you, your friends, and even your family will not always understand God's leading in your life. You cannot let their thoughts and opinions hinder you from obeying God's direction. Remember the truths of Proverbs 3:5-6. When God has another plan, be like Mary and Joseph and trust and obey!

A THRILL OF

Hope

Verse

Devotion

The Thrill of Victory

By Debra Lynn Birner

Nay, in all these things we are more than conquerors through him that loved us.

Romans 8:37

A baby born to a virgin! Matthew 1:23 "Behold, a virgin shall be with child, and shall bring forth a son, and they shall call his name Emmanuel, which being interpreted is, God with us."

Shepherds visited by angels! Luke 2:8-11 "And there were in the same country shepherds abiding in the field, keeping watch over their flock by night. And, lo, the angel of the Lord came upon them, and the glory of the Lord shone round about them: and they were sore afraid. And the angel said unto them, Fear not: for, behold, I bring you good tidings of great joy, which shall be to all people. For unto you is born this day in the city of David a Saviour, which is Christ the Lord."

God appearing in flesh! What a thrill! After 400 years of silence, God is speaking to His people again. He is providing Himself a sacrifice. We, a people with no hope, now have all the hope in the

We, a people
with no hope,
now have all
the hope in
the world!

world! John 1:14 "And the Word was made flesh, and dwelt among us, (and we beheld his glory, the glory as of the only begotten of the Father,) full of grace and truth."

What a change! Nothing would ever be the same again! Ephesians 2:12 "That at that time ye were without Christ, being aliens from the commonwealth of Israel, and strangers from the covenants of promise, having no hope, and without God in the world:"

When I was young, my Dad would watch the Wide World of Sports every week, and I wanted to be with my Dad, so I was right there watching it too (though I was not a sports fan). The program would start with some great sports victory, like a clip of someone winning the Olympics, and be followed up with some devastating clip, like a guy on skis tumbling down the mountain – and the announcer would proclaim: "The thrill of victory, and the agony of defeat!" What a contrast!

What does this have to do with Christmas (other than the snow-covered mountain the skier toppled down)? Well, Christmas is the greatest thrill of victory there is! Isaiah 9:6 "For unto us a child is born, unto us a son is given: and the government shall be upon his shoulder: and his name shall be called Wonderful, Counsellor, The mighty God, The everlasting Father, The Prince of Peace."

And, as for the agony of defeat – because of Christmas, because of the birth of our Saviour, because of His sacrifice on the cross, because of His great love for us ... we never have to suffer defeat. We have a guaranteed victory! Romans 8:37 "Nay, in all these things we are more than conquerors through him that loved us."

The best way to celebrate this Christmas, to celebrate our Saviour coming into the world, light into darkness – the best way ... is to celebrate the victory we have in Christ, in the salvation He has provided.

Back to the agony of defeat – if we are now still in the throes of defeat, we can have victory – we can have the victory this Christmas – we can have the victory now. Rom. 10:9-10 "That if thou shalt confess with thy mouth the Lord Jesus, and shalt believe in thine heart that God hath raised him from the dead, thou shalt be saved. For with the heart man believeth unto righteousness; and with the mouth confession is made unto salvation."

A thrill of hope, the weary world rejoices – Rejoice – The Thrill of Victory! Matthew 1:21 "And she shall bring forth a son, and thou shalt call his name JESUS: for he shall save his people from their sins." 1 Corinthians 15:57 " But thanks be to God, which giveth us the victory through our Lord Jesus Christ."

There may not be peace everywhere on earth, but we can have peace in our hearts.John 16:33 "These things I have spoken unto you, that in me ye might have peace. In the world ye shall have tribulation: but be of good cheer; I have overcome the world." Now that's the thrill of victory for sure!

A THRILL OF

Hope

Verse

Devotion

Making Memories

By Nicole Redmon

But Mary kept all these things, and pondered them in her heart.

Luke 2:19

Don't you just love Christmas time? I cannot think of one thing about Christmas that I do not enjoy. Well, maybe the dishes after a huge Christmas gathering! But, oh, to have friends and family to serve things on those dirty dishes makes the scrubbing well worth it! I can do lots of thinking and remembering while making those dishes clean again.

I wonder, sometimes, what Mary pondered on the most from that glorious night that our Saviour was born. Was it the long trip back to Bethlehem, or how her precious child was lying in a manger? Did she often reach back into her memories and grab the one where the angel of the Lord appeared to her to tell her she had been chosen by God to be the mother of Jesus, or maybe the memory of how the shepherds came running to find Him, and then to joyously spread the news of His coming? I guess I will never really know exactly, but it is fun to wonder sometimes.

97

The day that your sins were washed away and you became a new creature in Christ Jesus is the greatest memory ever made.

I love it when my mind allows me to remember a special Christmas memory. The memories from how we grew up and all the traditions we made and kept over the years are the best parts of the holiday season for me. All it takes is a quick trip around the living room with an old family photo album, and the Christmas stories start flying! I laugh until I am crying and cry until I'm laughing again! We learn a lot about each other and those family members who have passed away, too. (This is usually when those tears show up.)

Not only do I enjoy remembering special memories, but I love to make new ones too! I always tell my kiddos to have fun and make some memories! Then we can sit around and tell them to one another as the years go by. But there is one memory that I pray that you will forever be able to remember, and I pray that you will tell it, and tell it often, not just at Christmas time. Do you remember the day that you got saved? The day that your sins were washed away and you became a new creature in Christ Jesus? You see, my friend, that is the greatest memory ever made and told! I hope you can remember that time when you called on God to save you. If you have not made that memory, then today is the day you can become gloriously born again! And for those of you who are a child of God, I pray that you are telling that memory, especially to your family. What torment it is for those friends and family who say goodbye to you, not knowing if they will ever see you in Heaven. I know it is only possible for me to know for sure that I am born again, but I hope I have left enough "spiritual" memories for my kiddos to think back on and remember that their mama walked with God. I hope they can remember times when the Lord brought us through a trial or two, or where our faith in Him stayed true and He blessed us for it. I pray that they can remember Daddy and Mama testifying of His saving grace with tears rolling down their faces. Or maybe a time when they slipped into your room without knocking and caught you pouring your heart out to Jesus.

So, I ask you this Christmas season...what kind of memories have you made? What kind of memories are you making? Not all memories are good, I understand that. But I hope that you have made the most important thing in your life a memory. Give your heart and life to the Saviour ... ponder it often, and then, go tell it!

A THRILL OF

Hope

Verse

Devotion

When Your World Is Turned Upside Down

By Marsha Leto

For with God nothing shall be impossible.

Luke 1:37

Mary was in love. She was preparing to marry the man of her dreams. No doubt she imagined their future together — sharing meals, raising children, and building a home with Joseph, the man she was betrothed to.

But everything changed the day the angel appeared and said: "And, behold, thou shalt conceive in thy womb, and bring forth a son, and call his name JESUS." Luke 1:31

Her dreams suddenly turned into real-life drama. How would she explain this to Joseph, to her parents, to her friends? Would they believe her?

She faced:

- Deep uncertainty
- The threat of public shame
- Unanswered questions
- A complete detour from everything she planned

Have you ever been in a situation like this? Life is smooth and easy — and then your whole world is turned upside down.

- A phone call saying a loved one has passed away
- A cancer diagnosis
- A wayward child
- A financial crisis
- A broken relationship
- Something you never saw coming

You are left stunned, fearful, and unsure of what comes next. These may have been the same emotions Mary experienced. Let us look at the Scriptures to see how Mary responded when her life was being turned upside down.

1. Mary Trusted God's Word

Luke 1:38 " ... be it unto me according to thy word...."

- Mary didn't panic or run.
- Even though it seemed like an impossible situation, she trusted God.
- Mary did not understand everything in the beginning; she just trusted God.
- Mary knew God could be trusted.
- Trust means to fully rely on.
- Mary was fully relying on God and that His plan was the best.

2. Mary Believed in God's Power

Luke 1:37 "For with God nothing shall be impossible."

- Mary knew that what the angel promised was humanly impossible – but not with God.
- Mary knew only God and His power could do such a thing.
- We have an almighty, powerful God Who can do anything!

3. Mary Walked in Humility

Luke 1:38 "And Mary said, Behold the handmaid of the Lord;"

- Mary calls herself a handmaid, a servant.
- Mary is revealing that she is submissive to God's plan.
- Mary was willing to let go of what she thought she should look like and follow God's plan.

4. Mary Knew the Scriptures

- Mary no doubt heard the Scriptures read regularly at home and in the temple.
- She alludes to many verses in the Old Testament.
- Her song of praise in Luke 1:46-55 is like Hannah's prayer in I Samuel 2.
- When life got uncertain, God's Word came alive in her heart.

5. Mary Had Courage

- She risked her life, her reputation, and her relationships, yet she obeyed.
- True courage is doing what's right, even when it costs something.

6. Mary Praised God in the Storm

Luke 1:46-47 "And Mary said, My soul doth magnify the Lord, and my spirit hath rejoiced in God my Saviour."

- Mary didn't wait for everything to make sense.
- She praised Him in confusion.
- She rejoiced in God's goodness.
- She accepted her new role as a life-changing blessing.

7. Mary Realized This Life Change Was a Blessing

Luke 1:48... "from henceforth all generations shall call me blessed."

- Mary went from being a humble handmaiden to being remembered throughout all history as Jesus' mother.
- What a way to be remembered! All because she was willing to accept God's plan.

How will you respond when your world is turned upside down? Will you trust God's plan, like Mary did? Will you believe in His power, even when it feels impossible? Will you walk in humility, know His Word, and praise Him – even when it's hard?

Times were difficult, but she knew her Bible, and she continued until she could praise God for the turn-my-world-upside-down life-changing event – the one we now call Christmas. "For unto you is born this day in the city of David a Saviour, who is Christ the Lord." Luke 2:11

Hope

Verse

Devotion

A Modern-Day Mary

By Rainy Lehman

And the angel said unto her, Fear not, Mary: for thou hast found favour with God.

Luke 1:30

Imagine for a moment that God was choosing a mother for Jesus today, a woman to raise the Saviour of the world – not in first-century Nazareth, but in the noise and chaos of our modern lives. What kind of woman would He look for?

I believe He would scroll past the influencers and executives, the athletes and actresses, and land on someone unnoticed by the world, yet noticed by heaven. Could that woman be you? Mary was young, poor, and from a town with no reputation. Yet God saw her as highly favored. She was not chosen for her status, talents, or accomplishments, but for her heart.

Before we go further, it's important to remember: Mary was not divine. God never intended for her to be worshipped. She was fully human – a sinner, like the rest of us, in need of a Saviour. In Luke 1:47, she herself declared, "And my spirit hath rejoiced

in God my Saviour'. Yet despite her humanity, she stands as one of the most remarkable women in Scripture — a beautiful example of godly character, courage, and faith. As we look at her life, we're not exalting Mary, but exalting the God who worked through her, and asking: If God were looking for a modern-day Mary, would He find one in me?

Let's take a closer look at Mary's life and heart and consider three attributes that made her a vessel for God's greatest mission— attributes we can all seek to cultivate.

A Heart of Humble Surrender

"And Mary said, Behold the handmaid of the Lord; be it unto me according to thy word. And the angel departed from her."
Luke 1:38

Mary's response to the angel wasn't one of negotiation or fear. She didn't ask, "How will this affect my reputation? What will people say?" She simply said yes. True surrender is not passive resignation — it is active trust. Mary willingly gave up control of her life to embrace God's plan, even though it meant risk, ridicule, and radical change. Would we be willing to say yes to God without seeing the full picture? To be misunderstood for obedience? To carry something Holy that may cost us comfort? Modern-day Marys are women who surrender fully — trusting God's purpose over personal plans.

She was not chosen for her status or talents but for her heart.

A Life of Quiet Faithfulness

"But Mary kept all these things, and pondered them in her heart."
Luke 2:19

Mary's strength was not loud or showy. She did not seek attention or recognition. She pondered. She listened. She obeyed in the ordinary.

In a world that glorifies loudness and visibility, Mary's quiet faithfulness stands in contrast. She lived her "yes" to God, not just once at the angel's visit, but every day – through childbirth in a stable, through exile, through raising a perfect Son in an imperfect world.

A modern-day Mary is not someone who needs a platform, but someone faithful in the unseen places. The kitchen table, the workplace, the late-night prayer for a child – these become sacred spaces when lived for God's glory.

A Spirit of Reverent Praise

"And Mary said, My soul doth magnify the Lord, and my spirit hath rejoiced in God my Saviour."
Luke 1:46-47

Mary didn't exalt herself – she magnified the Lord. Her life is a beautiful declaration of God's faithfulness and mercy.

Even in uncertainty, Mary chose worship. Even in confusion, she trusted His goodness. Her praise wasn't dependent on perfect circumstances but flowed from a deep well of belief in God's character.

Modern-day Marys are women who praise before the breakthrough, who lift their eyes even when life is heavy, and who make much of Jesus no matter the stage of the story.

God is still looking for vessels today — not to carry the physical Christ, but to carry His message, His love, His truth to a world that desperately needs it. He's not searching for perfection, but for posture — women whose hearts are surrendered, whose lives are faithful, and whose spirits magnify Him.

Would He choose me? Would He choose you? May we live in such a way that heaven would say of us, "Fear not, _____: for thou hast found favour with God."

A THRILL OF

Hope

Verse

Devotion

Choose to Believe!

By Lydia L. Riley

And blessed is she that believed: for there shall be a performance of those things which were told her from the Lord.

Luke 1:45

These words came from a Spirit-filled older lady (Elisabeth) as an encouragement to a godly young lady (Mary) whose whole world had just been turned upside down by an angelic message. This is one of the few Bible verses that uses feminine pronouns: "... blessed is she that believed: for there shall be a performance of those things which were told her from the Lord." Ladies, this is like our very own special Bible verse to claim!

This verse jumped off the pages of my Bible about two years ago during a message being preached from these well-known chapters – How had I never quite "seen" this verse before?! These words became deeply embedded in my own heart as a promise of hope – for the Lord had recently asked of me some things that seemed overwhelming and nearly impossible; yet I knew that it was His still small voice that had spoken to my heart, asking for my obedience. Soon after initial steps of faith in this new direction, my world had been turned upside down with what many would call a catastrophe, and God had begun writing an entirely new chapter in my life. This verse offered such joy and anticipation that my God would perform the things He had whispered into my soul and would bless my simple faith and steps of obedience.

I didn't have to understand all His plan or all that He was requiring of me; I was to simply trust and obey and leave the performance (the results) to Him. "I will cry unto God most high; unto God that performeth all things for me." Psalm 57:2

I have found that the beginning of a new journey, a new chapter, or uncharted territory through which God is leading can usually be described in two words – terrifying (I'm crying to You God!) and exhilarating (I'm watching You perform miracles for me God!) all at the same time. Choose to believe God! Has the Lord spoken to your heart about a task He is asking you to fulfill? Is there something He is asking you to believe Him for, even though it seems impossible? You might be scared. That's okay. Do it scared! Choose to believe!

Do not be inhibited by your insignificance, by the impossibilities, or by the improbable – "for with God nothing shall be impossible." Luke 1:37. He is the One who works miracles. Remember that God often chooses the insignificant when accomplishing the impossible.

Put yourself into Mary's shoes for just a bit of time. Imagine her thoughts and feelings:

- Her reputation was at stake (Matthew 1:18)
  ... She chose to believe God.

- Her relationships were nearly severed (Matthew 1:19)
  ... She chose to believe God.

- She faced the risk of separation (Matthew 1:19)
  ... She chose to believe God.

- Her reality seemed surreal (Matthew 1:20-21)
  ... She chose to believe God.

- Her role was sacred (Luke 1:35)
  ... She chose to believe God.

- Her rejoicing was in her Saviour (Luke 1:46-49)
  ... She chose to believe God.

- She remembered the Scriptures (Luke 1:55)
  ... She chose to believe God.

- She reflected in silence (Luke 2:19)
  ... She chose to believe God.

- Her response to suffering (Luke 2:35, John 19:25)
  ... She chose to believe God.

Mary surrendered her life, her own will, her unknown future, and all her aspirations with the words "Behold the handmaid of the Lord; be it unto me according to thy word." Luke 1:38a.

What is in your hand to give to the Lord? What is He asking you to do for His work? What dreams has he placed within your heart to accomplish for His kingdom? Remember to be faithful in the little things – He chooses the small people (a young virgin) in small places (Bethlehem) to bring small things (a tiny little baby) into the world that are eternally life-changing! Choose to believe! For there shall be a performance of those things which were told you from the Lord!

A THRILL OF

Hope

Verse

Devotion

Hope beyond Christmas

By Sarah Russell

Which hope we have as an anchor of the soul, both sure and stedfast....

Hebrews 6:19a

The Christmas hymn, O Holy Night, surprisingly doesn't have its origins in the Baptist faith, nor was its author a believer in Jesus Christ! It was written in 1843 by Placid Cappeau, a French poet, commissioned by a Catholic priest to write a Christmas hymn to be sung at Christmas Mass. Its words were written by a man who claimed no faith!

It was later set to music by a Jewish man who was also not a believer! And an interesting fact is that it was the very first song to be played over radio waves in 1906. But despite the hymn's origin and history, it does hold within it some poetic truths about the birth of our Saviour. One of those lines is "a thrill of hope." And, oh, indeed, the birth of Christ did bring about a thrill of hope to those who experienced and heard about His remarkable entrance into our world. Many had been looking for the coming of the Saviour and were waiting in hope for His arrival. And then, He came! The thrill of hope they must have felt. Mary,

The hope of assurance that my God holds me and keeps me.

Joseph, the shepherds, Simeon, Anna, and the wise men knew the blessed Hope had come. What a thrill!

The word "hope" is used a lot during the Christmas season. It's on cards, wrapping papers, written in lovely flowing script on brightly colored glass ornaments. But most souls have no idea what and Who the real Hope is!

We, as believers, know the only real hope in this world is Jesus Christ. He is the greatest hope this world has ever known. But our hope goes beyond the hope of Christ's birth. God's Word gives us so much more to hope for.

In Colossians 1:23, we see the "hope of the gospel." This hope is the most important one of all. This is the hope we need to redeem our souls. Without it, we would be most miserable in this world. Our salvation is only through the hope of the Gospel of Jesus Christ. Have you experienced the Hope of the Gospel? If not, I invite you to experience this hope for yourself.

In Titus 2:13, we are given "hope of eternal life"! That is an amazing hope! I've talked with my young children about this hope many times. Their little hearts cannot yet grasp the concept that this life here dims in comparison to our eternal life after death. I cannot fully grasp the glorious reality of our life to come. This life is just the beginning. What hope!

In Hebrews 6:17-20, our hearts leap at the hope set before us. A reiteration of our previous hopes (salvation and eternal life) and the fact that our God is unchangeable, trustworthy, and incapable of deceit. What a thrill of hope I feel when I think of the anchor that keeps my soul. The hope of assurance that my God holds me and keeps me.

In 1 Peter 1:13, we see a very special hope that every believer should be looking for. The Hope of the revelation of Jesus Christ. We are looking now for this blessed hope. The revealing of our Saviour in the clouds. I'm speaking of course of the Second Coming of the King. The hope it brings to believers in turn brings fear to the unbeliever. But we have a thrill of hope in this. That our Lord has not forgotten His people. And that any day now we will hear Him call us home. What a thrill it would be to spend Christmas bowing before the King of Kings instead of kneeling before our Christmas trees, passing out gifts. Now that's something to hope for!

I sure am thankful for the hope God's Word gives me! I encourage you to open His Word this Christmas season. Open it like the gift that it is and take from it the beautiful hopes that He has for each of us. And in this busy time of year, I pray each of us would take the time to sit still in the quiet, to be a part of the silent night and listen to our blessed Hope, our Saviour who made Heaven and nature sing, to hear His voice and experience that thrill of Hope that only He can bring.

A THRILL OF

Hope

Verse

Devotion

A Uniquely Perfect Gift

By Callie Payne

Now concerning spiritual gifts, brethren, I would not have you ignorant.

1 Corinthians 12:1

As Christmas gets closer, we really get excited about picking out the perfect gift for all the people on our list. We want to get them something personal, something that is "just them" when we see it. We want to get something that maybe they can use day to day or have been wanting for a while... Whatever it may be, we want to get that special someone a memorable gift, letting them know we care. We don't always look at our list and decide to bulk order the exact item to give everyone. I'm going to go out on a limb and say that there isn't a universal gift that would just fit everyone's needs and wants each year. No! We enjoy taking the time to look and dig to find something different, unique, and special!

This is how God divided our gifts to the church! Different gifts for each of us! Something that was tailored to each person. I Corinthians 12 is all about the diversity of gifts God intended for us, and how we all

Comparison will steal your joy faster than just about anything...

fit together as the body of Christ. I Corinthians 12:12 says, "For as the body is one, and hath many members, and all the members of that one body, being many, are one body: so also is Christ."

We don't have the same gift as our sisters in Christ around us have. Although it's a very human reaction, we aren't supposed to be comparing the gifts they do or don't have to what we do or don't have. You may look across the pew and see your sister in Christ excel in an area that God didn't intend for you to minister in. You may see a Sunday school teacher and think to yourself a thought of comparison - although not always negative towards them - you may wish for a ministry or a role for yourself. But Satan uses that critical or comparison thought pattern to steal the blessing and joy out of the ministry He has placed you in.

Comparison will steal your joy faster than just about anything... "Neither give place to the devil." Ephesians 4:27

You don't see what goes on behind the scenes of others' ministries. Whether you think they need to do more like you or wish you could be involved in what they're doing, remember God has a specific, special ministry and spiritual gift that He has uniquely picked out for you. He knows what you can do with it. It is your job to steward it and not let it collect dust. That talent, special skill, ministry- start using your gift He's designed. Don't let comparing and contrasting cause you to doubt or bring contention into your church, home, and ministry. I Corinthians 12:25 "That there should be no schism in the body; but that the members should have the same care one for another."

This Christmas season, identify what gifts God has blessed you with and use them for His glory. Don't let yourself envy someone's position or criticize what you feel they "should" be doing or not doing.

In I Corinthians 12:22-26, we see God describe the many different members of one body with words and phrases such as "necessary," "more abundant comliness," and "abundant honour."

Make a brief list of ways you can use the gifts and ministry God has custom-made for you. Find ways you can use it and "exercise" it in this upcoming new year. As you look at your "gift list" from God, let it encourage you that God took the time to pick something out just to fit you, your talents, and personality. Let that bless your heart and bring you not only closer to Him, but also to your church family. We are all the body of Christ as Ephesians says, "From whom the whole body fitly joined together and compacted by that which every joint supplieth, according to the effectual working in the measure of every part, maketh increase of the body unto the edifying of itself in love." Ephesians 4:16

A THRILL OF

Hope

Verse

Devotion

The Ideal Christmas

By Renee Patton

Thanks be unto God for his unspeakable gift.

II Corinthians 9:15

What is an ideal Christmas? Better yet, what does it look like? We all have different renditions of trees, lights, family, and festivities! Do you go caroling, drive through lighted neighborhoods? Make a cocoa bar and decorate Christmas cookies? Do you make brownies after the tree is decorated?

Each year, as Christmas approaches, I find myself reflecting on what truly makes this season "ideal." For many, it is the anticipation of laughter echoing through decorated halls, the scent of cinnamon and pine, and the warmth of family gathered close. Yet, life's seasons shift, and the picture of the perfect holiday is often painted with brushstrokes of longing and change. We treasure traditions, but sometimes circumstances require us to let go and embrace a new kind of celebration — one that is quieter, but no less meaningful.

Is this Christmas going to be the first where "ideal" is far from reality? Perhaps you are alone for the first time. Maybe your children

The ideal Christmas comes with our hearts turned toward the Lord.

cannot come home for the first time, or it has been many years since they have been home for Christmas? For myself, all my children are married and serving God in various regions. The "ideal" Christmas, where everyone is all home at the same time, may only happen once a decade.

Has your ideal Christmas fallen apart? Please, do not despair! God is there! Always there for you! I love the verse Jeremiah 29:11, "For I know the thoughts that I think toward you, saith the LORD, thoughts of peace, and not of evil, to give you an expected end." In our finite minds, we tend to define "expected end" as what we see or need and not what God sees for us. Change is hard. Some changes are good and exciting. Other changes are hard and taxing. Whatever change has come your way, embrace change with grace ... grace to yourself! God's grace is sufficient! Allow God to keep you under His wings. Endure tough days by focusing on others, and your own challenges will feel less significant.

As things change, look for the true spirit of Christmas in simple moments. This may be a quiet phone call with a distant loved one, a handwritten card, or the soft glow of a single candle flickering with hope in the dark. The absence of familiar faces at the table can leave an ache, but it can also open our eyes to unexpected blessings — a neighbor's kindness, the steady companionship of faith, the peace that settles when we remember we are never truly alone.

The trappings of Christmas — gifts, gatherings, and traditions — are precious, but they are not the source of the season's joy. If we listen closely, we may hear God's still, small voice reminding us that love itself is the greatest tradition, and that our celebrations, no matter how modest, are enough when they are offered with gratitude and a spirit of giving.

Sometimes, the journey to an "ideal" Christmas leads us inward, past the noise and the traditions, to a place of gentle surrender. We may find ourselves setting aside the familiar trappings of the season to make room for something deeper — a quiet trust that even in disappointment or solitude, there is a gift waiting to be unwrapped. This gift does not come in a brightly colored box or with a bow, but in the assurance that God sees us, knows our needs, and meets us right where we are.

Remember, the ideal Christmas comes with our hearts turned toward the Lord. It is He who gives us the unspeakable gift of grace (II Corinthians 9:15). Paul reminds the Corinthians to exhort others, sow bountifully, and give cheerfully. Then, God's unspeakable gift of grace will follow (II Corinthians 9). Traditions change and expectations may go unmet, yet God gives grace to embrace and find meaning in simple moments and recognize that the true spirit of Christmas lies in love, gratitude, and faith. Even in solitude or disappointment, God's presence and grace offer hope. The ideal Christmas is found not in perfect circumstances, but in grateful hearts seeking His unspeakable gift.

A THRILL OF

Hope

Verse

Devotion

Christmas Hope:
Trusting the God Who Keeps His Word

By Hannah Hyatt

Now all this was done, that it might be fulfilled which was spoken of the Lord by the prophet, saying, Behold, a virgin shall be with child, and shall bring forth a son, and they shall call his name Emmanuel, which being interpreted is, God with us.

Matthew 1:22-23

Hope. We sometimes use the word flippantly or as a synonym for wish or desire. "I hope these cookies turn out okay," or "I hope we can finish school at a decent time today" – we've all been there! But hope is much more than that. Webster's 1828 dictionary defines hope as "confidence in a future event; the highest degree of well-founded expectation of good; as a hope founded on God's gracious promises; a scriptural sense." Our hope is not just wishful thinking that everything will somehow work out. Instead, it is a steady confidence anchored in the unshakable promises of God. Life is filled with hard seasons of pain, uncertainty, loss, and waiting that can feel endless and overwhelming. Yet as believers, we are never left to face those seasons alone or without hope.

This kind of hope is rooted in God's proven faithfulness. The same God who kept His promise by sending His Son into the world at Christmas continues to sustain us in every trial. His fulfilled promise in Christ's first coming assures us that His promise of Christ's return is equally certain. Because God has already proven Himself faithful to keep His Word, we can trust Him with our present struggles and our future.

Hope Fulfilled at Christmas

Christmas itself is proof that God keeps His promises. Over thousands of years, the coming of Jesus had been prophesied. In both Matthew 1 and Luke 1-2, we are reminded that the birth of Jesus had been foretold by the prophets. One of my favorite phrases in the Christmas story is found in Matthew 1:22, "Now all this was done, that it might be fulfilled..." For centuries, God's people waited for the Messiah, and in the manger of Bethlehem, God proved that He is faithful to keep His Word.

The birth of Jesus fulfilled the hope for those who had been looking for Him, but it also gives hope to the world today. Galatians 4:4-6 tells us, "But when the fulness of the time was come, God sent forth his Son, made of a woman, made under the law, To redeem them that were under the law, that we might receive the adoption of sons. And because ye are sons, God hath sent forth the Spirit of his Son into your hearts, crying, Abba, Father." Because Christ came, we can be redeemed from our sinful state and made a part of God's family.

Hope Found in Tribulation

"Therefore being justified by faith, we have peace with God through our Lord Jesus Christ: By whom also we have access by faith into this grace wherein we stand, and rejoice in hope of the glory of God. And not only so, but we glory in tribulations also: knowing that tribulation worketh patience; And patience, experience; and experience, hope: And hope maketh not ashamed; because the love of God is shed abroad in our hearts by the Holy Ghost which is given unto us." Romans 5:1-5

In these verses, Paul reminds us of the good things we have through Jesus Christ – peace with and access to God, grace, and hope. He goes on to say that because of these blessings, we can glory in tribulations because they produce good fruit in us. I love that there are no coincidences in the Bible. We've already seen that hope is an expected outcome, and Paul states here that experience produces hope. We can look back over our lives and see where God has answered prayer, worked in situations, and met our needs, and confidently expect that He will do it again. Not only do we have personal experience, but we can look in the Bible, history, and the lives of others and see where God has always done what He said He would do. Experience tells us we can have hope. The phrase "hope maketh not ashamed" simply means that the hope we have in Christ will not put us to shame or disappoint us; it will always be fulfilled and accomplish His will in our lives.

Our trials are not wasted. Romans 8:28-29 assures us of this, "And we know that all things work together for good to them that love God, to them who are the called according to his purpose. For whom he did foreknow, he also did predestinate to be conformed to the image of his Son, that he might be the firstborn among many brethren." All things, good and bad, are for my good and His glory. We can confidently hope in the fact that God is shaping us, strengthening us, and anchoring us deeper in His love through tribulations.

Hope Foreseen in the Rapture

While I am thankful for the hope I have in Christ in this present life, I am so glad that He has given us a future hope as well. Titus 2:13 says we are to be, "Looking for that blessed hope, and the glorious appearing of the great God and our Saviour Jesus Christ..." That will be a wonderful day for those who know the Lord!

In Romans 8:18, Paul tells us that our future is so much better than anything this life has to offer, "For I reckon that the sufferings of this present time are not worthy to be compared with the glory which shall be revealed in us." The glory that will be revealed in us is that we will be like Christ. I John 3:2-3, "Beloved, now are we the sons of God, and it doth not yet appear what we shall be: but we know that, when he shall appear, we shall be like him; for we shall see him as he is. And every man that hath this hope in him purifieth himself, even as he is pure." The hope of the Rapture should motivate us to live a life that is pleasing to God today. Paul refers to this struggle later on in Romans 8:22-25, where he links the coming of Christ to hope, "For we know that the whole creation groaneth and travaileth in pain together until now. And not only they, but ourselves also, which have the firstfruits of the Spirit, even we ourselves groan within ourselves, waiting for the adoption, to wit, the redemption of our body. For we are saved by hope: but hope that is seen is not hope: for what a man seeth, why doth he yet hope for? But if we hope for that we see not, then do we with patience wait for it." The groaning of creation and the groaning in our hearts remind us that this world is broken, but not forever. A day is coming when Christ will return, when the bondage of corruption will give way to glorious liberty. What a day that will be!

Conclusion

The hope of Christmas is not just an event to celebrate once a year - it is a perpetual reminder of God's faithfulness. We can trust that the same God who worked through thousands of years and countless lives to bring Jesus into the world at just the right place and the right time is able and faithful to sustain us through our trials. Because He has already kept this promise, we can trust Him with every burden we carry and every tomorrow we cannot see.

Our hope is not without a foundation. It is anchored in the unchanging character of God and strengthened each time we recall His past faithfulness - both in Scripture and in our own lives. Every answered prayer, every provision, and every situation when His grace has sustained us is a reminder that He will keep every future promise as well. So, whether you find yourself celebrating joys, enduring tribulation, or longing for Christ's appearing, you will not be disappointed. He has been faithful, He is faithful now, and He will always be faithful. Whatever you are facing, remember you can have hope because God keeps His promises. We can have confidence in the present and look with confidence to the future because our hope is found in the One who never fails.

A THRILL OF

Hope

Verse

Devotion

Until He Comes

By Cherith Shiflett

Then we which are alive and remain shall be caught up together with them in the clouds, to meet the Lord in the air: and so shall we ever be with the Lord.

1 Thessalonians 4:17

At this time of year, my thoughts naturally turn towards the birth of Jesus. It's one of my favorite passages in the Bible. Every time I read it, I feel a surge of joy and hope. It truly is such a special story.

Recently, I've been mulling over the phrase "Until He Comes."

This led me to meditate on the first time He came. Did you know there were 400 years of silence between the last recorded prophecy of His coming in the Old Testament and the time of His actual birth? Four hundred years. That is a long time to wait. Not only was it a long time to wait, but for many, Jesus' birth was their only hope.

I taught World History for a few years. One of the reasons I enjoyed teaching history was that you truly see "His story" entwined throughout time. Even though there were 400 years of spiritual silence, these years were not silent historically. Many wars, exiles, conflicts, and changes of rulers took place. There was great oppression - especially

149

Until He comes, we should be walking holy and set apart.

for anyone who still believed in a coming Messiah. In 63 B.C, Roman rule came into play, setting the stage for the birth of Jesus, but I'm sure the ones waiting had no idea what was about to happen. In my mind, I see a group of people who passed on to their generations the tale of a coming Messiah. Not only this, they also pored over and studied the prophetic books. They knew He was coming. They had no idea God was preparing the world for His coming in several ways- a common language, a vast road system (for spreading the Gospel), and a widespread knowledge of the Bible. During this time, the OT was accessible to the common people. Even Gentiles could read of a Promised Messiah.

They didn't know all of this was happening behind the scenes. They just knew He was coming.

Galatians 4:4 says, "But when the fulness of the time was come, God sent forth his Son, made of a woman, made under the law." When the fullness of time was complete, Jesus came as a baby. He fulfilled every hope and desire of the ones who longed for His coming. Can you imagine the joy that was sparked in those who had faithfully believed all those years?

Let's put this in perspective for today. We're in the same position as those during the 400 silent years. We know Jesus is coming back. We have studied and pored over the prophecies. There is no doubt in our minds, Jesus is coming back. We have no idea when. But, could it be that God is preparing the world for His Second Coming, just as He did all those years ago? I believe so. And once again, in the fullness of time, He will come! I Thessalonians 4:16–17 says "For the Lord himself shall descend from heaven with a shout, with the voice of the archangel, and with the trump of God: and the dead in Christ shall rise first: Then we which are alive and remain shall be caught up together with them in the clouds, to meet the Lord in the air: and so shall we ever be with the Lord."

This is an amazing promise, but until He comes, we should work faithfully in His service (I Peter 4:7). Until He comes, we should be willing to build up one another and encourage (Hebrews 10:24-25). Until He comes, we should be witnessing to every creature (Acts 1:8). Until He comes, we should be walking holy and set apart. (II Peter 3:11-12) Until He comes, we should be watching and waiting. (Matthew 24:42)

A personal favorite song comes to my mind.

"Until He comes, I'll love Him though I may not see. My broken heart and bitter tears are good for me, and the darkest valley may be left to walk before I'm home, but I'll take it to Calvary until He comes.

There'll be times I'll walk alone, and dark nights I'll cry and I'll wonder if I'll ever smile again, but I refuse to turn around or lay my armour down until He comes again."

Friend, let's not lay down our armor. Now is not the time to give in and give up. Now is the time to endure - until He comes.

A THRILL OF

Hope

Verse

Devotion

About The Authors

Each author has been handpicked because of their testimony
for Christ. God has gifted each writer with incredibly versatile
perspectives of the Christian life. These godly ladies come
from all walks of life including pastor's wives and daughters,
missionary wives, church staff ladies, and faithful
church members. Their written words of wisdom
are sure to bless your heart.

To know more about our writers please visit:
thehighlyfavouredlife.com/our-story